The Learning Curve
Lessons on
Life Love and Laundry

Cindy Gregg

Meyer Publishing House

Printed in the United States of America

Library of Congress Catalog Card Number: 97-94362
ISBN: 0-9660006-0-9

Cover art and design: Sylvia Rudolph
Interior design: Mori Studio

Meyer Publishing House
27 East 54th Street
Minneapolis, MN 55419
(612) 823-4167

Dedicated To
Four From Whom
I've Learned
My Parents, Henry and Mildred
My Children, Wayne and Kim

Acknowledgments

Heartfelt thanks to the following people for their encouragement and support: my editor, Margie Adler, my parents, Henry and Mildred Meyer, my children, Wayne and Kim Gregg, and my dear friends, Versea Bourdaghs, Bert Doyle, Joe DeLorme, Mary Hanson, Susan Jenkins, Judy Jones, Judy Rae, Sylvia Rudolph, Leslie Stevenson and Pam Wynn.

INTRODUCTION

From kindergarten to college I settled into the curved, seated posture of learning. In classroom after classroom I dutifully listened, took notes, raised my hand, spoke and learned. After college I precariously positioned myself in front of a class full of antsy first graders, transformed suddenly from the one who absorbs knowledge to the one who imparts it.

Life, of course, is not that simple a dichotomy. I continued to learn from experiences in the classroom and everywhere else. At fifty, I am learning still, and I hope that I never stop. Learning makes my life dynamic.

Sometimes lessons rise quickly and quietly, like fragrant bread dough doubling its girth within hours in my small kitchen. Other times they barge in with loud clanging sounds, like the "music" my kids used to make when they turned pots, pans and wooden spoons into a spirited percussion band.

Whatever shape, size or decibel level they come in, lessons eventually enrich my life. In the pages ahead I reflect and stop along the path my life has taken, along what I call my learning curve. I hope that as you read my reflections, you smile knowingly, laugh liberally and connect contentedly with your own.

TABLE OF CONTENTS

Letting Go

Seasons, Sizes, Samplers and Stills

Megamalls, Melanin and Men

Don't Fence Me In

Past, Present, Future

Object Lessons

LETTING GO

BOXES

They're a part of our lives, from the very small ones that cushion jewelry to the very large ones we inhabit and call homes. The ones that fascinate me the most, though, are the invisible ones, the boxes we build in our minds to define and confine ourselves and others.

Putting people in boxes is a kind of reflex action of mine. Shortly after I meet them, I formulate an opinion and hurriedly file them in an imaginary sliding slot. One entire section of my brain is like the wall at the post office with varied first-impression boxes lining it from floor to ceiling.

Getting to know a person better sometimes confirms my initial hunch. However, what I really love is when this box making of mine gets turned on its ear. Every so often someone does something that in no way fits into the box I've built for them.

A few years ago I worked in the admitting department of a large city hospital, where some doctors were experimenting with a laser technique to remove tattoos. Occasionally, conversation with my co-workers veered off into the direction of would you or wouldn't you have a tattoo. On one particular day, Jeanne, a woman I didn't know very well, but for whom I had built and assigned a box, joined in the conversation.

She was a fidgety woman in her early forties who lived alone with her dog less than a mile from her parents. She was heavyset, Lutheran and prone to talking at length about aches and pains and recipes. I imagined Jeanne living in a small, conservative world devoid of any real adventure. Naturally, based on my rarely fallible first impression, I had decided already where she stood on the tattoo issue.

Suddenly, in the middle of this engrossing controversy to remove or not remove tattoos, Jeanne blurted out, "I don't know why someone would want to get their tattoo removed. I love mine and would never do that!"

Woa! It was blow me over with a feather time. "Excuse me," I felt like saying, "but I thought that I just heard you say..." Before I could, someone else asked where the tattoo was. Jeanne proudly pulled up the sleeve of her powder blue blouse, and there, for all the world to see, was a pink rose in full bloom, framed by three heart-shaped leaves. I thought I was hallucinating, but after blinking hard several times, the tattoo was still there.

Now, granted, as tattoos go, a pink rose would fall into the conservative category; but this was a category of *tattoos*. Jeanne had a *tattoo!* I suddenly realized that the box I'd put her in was the wrong box. Jeanne lived in a box where a visit to the tattoo parlor was acceptable. I was amazed. After that day, whenever I heard Jeanne talking about how long to bake blond brownies or the ache in her left shoulder, I'd say to myself, "Jeanne's got a tattoo!" I never did put her back in that box I'd built for her, the one I created before I got to view the bloom of her proud, pink rose.

ATTENTION SPAN

My attention span's not what it used to be. In college I flew through *War and Peace* in two sittings. Now I'm lucky if I get through the directions on my shampoo bottle without becoming distracted.

Signs of decline manifest themselves at other times, too. For instance, I may start out from the kitchen toward the living room with a clear mission in my mind. By the time I've reached the living room, I haven't a clue why I'm there. I bemoan my attention's teensy-weensy span measurable only in nano-seconds.

There are a couple of ways to handle this mind-turned-mush condition. You can learn one by watching cats. My cat will amble her way through a room and suddenly spot something of keen interest to her on a surface just a little too high for her to jump. She'll go for it anyway and miss. The thud to the floor is followed by an "Oh, that was part of my plan all along" expression as she saunters off without skipping a step. This technique elevates denial to an art form.

Another option is to adjust your attitude the way you adjust reading material to blend better with this time in your life. Men, sex and bikinis are pretty much gone; your memory is just following suit. So you switch from romances to mysteries (as in what *did* I want in the basement, what *was* my point in bringing that up?) Mutter to yourself something about the magnificent mystery of your mind, teasing you with beginnings for which it has absolutely no endings. Speaking of which, I think we've come to the end of this piece - and none too soon - my focus is beginning one of its infamous fades.

REIGNING CATS AND DOGS

On this rainy October day, I lounge in my favorite chair, the dog lying at my feet, the cat purring on the radiator. Suddenly I think of the phrase pairing weather and pets: raining cats and dogs. The phrase more suited to my experience with these creatures is *reigning* cats and dogs.

It particularly fits the majestic mindset of cats, who believe their destiny is to rule. The rules, which are made painfully clear from the beginning, go something like this:

You will at all times acknowledge my nobility and treat me with deference and devotion.

I invented independence - get over this bonding notion.

I require a throne. It may happen to be your favorite chair. Here's where that deference thing comes in.

There will be no talk of declawing. My need for freedom supercedes your need for decent-looking furniture.

Never utter the words "owning a pet." Owners are the ones that make the rules - enough said?

I could go on, but it only gets uglier. Any attempt to challenge the rules and you find your bed with its lovely Laura Ashley sheets turned suddenly into a litter box. We call this passive aggressive, they consider it pure genius.

You try guilting them, they counter with the gall (unmitigated variety) of not giving a damn. After having gone through the first three stages of grief (denial, anger, bargaining), you finally come to acceptance of your servile state, while developing a rich fantasy life in which you're wearing lots of domesticated fur. You've learned passive aggressive from the best of them.

HOT FLASHES

It hasn't always been this hot. After all, I was born in Iowa and have lived the past thirty years in Minnesota, second cousin to Siberia.

I knew I'd entered a new phase of my life when the temperature inside my body began bearing absolutely no resemblance to the temperature outside. On one refreshing January day when it was about 214 degrees below zero, I started sweating like Nixon during the "I am not a crook" speech. I hadn't recently committed some sleazy felony I was trying to cover up so I searched elsewhere for the answer.

Elsewhere turned out to be not about my actions but about my time. Parts of my body were sending powerful messages, letting me know they were in the process of shutting down. Sweet little ovaries were no longer interested in egg production. Like two worn out Easter bunnies they finally got fed up with years of clockwork compliance and said, "Enough is enough! We're done. We've worked hard for you for a long time, and now we're retiring. We're not moving to Florida, we'll still be here for you but only in the decorative sense, like the pointing, smiling women at a car show. "Well," I felt like saying, "I don't mind the shift, but as far as your method of notification is concerned, I'd have preferred a fax to these flashes.

Even though it seemed a little early for menopause (I was 40) I headed straight to the doctor and gave a little blood in exchange for a little information. The information indicated that I was indeed in the beginning stages of this new and mysterious phase of my life.

I'm a firm believer in getting help when needed, so when full- blown menopause hit, I discussed with my doctor the pros and cons of HRT (Hormone Replacement Therapy). In my particular situation, I concluded, the pros far outweighed the cons.

This therapy involves no couches, no $80/hour sessions, no locating my inner child. All I'm required to locate is my mouth, place in it a daily pill with a little water, and swallow. It's made my life easier. The pink flush to my cheeks now is Revlon, and I sweat when I'm exerting, not at the drop of some hormonally- imbalanced hat. Besides that, I'm greatly reducing my chance of heart disease, increasing my likelihood of keeping strong bones and skin that won't turn Saharan by the time I'm seventy. Hooray for HRT!

AA

Please prepare to put aside prejudice and pedantic protest as you consider the personal problem I place passionately before you. I know you'd never guess it, but I have a slight addiction to alliteration (is slight addiction an oxymoron?). I like variety in the rest of my life, but when it comes to stringing words together to make phrases, sentences, and paragraphs I seek a sameness in the starting syllables. It's gotten way out of hand, and I'm finally getting help.

I've started attending AA (Alliteraholics Anonymous) meetings. Hello, my name is Cindy and I'm an alliteraholic.

Woe, it felt so good to say it, to get that load off my chest! There are all sorts of people there. Some can *speak* forever without alliteration, but put a pen or pencil in their problematic little paws and all these people produce are preposterous poetry or prose. They can't bring themselves to write out a check where the amount isn't alliterate. It has to be twenty-two, fifty-five, ninety-nine, etc. They have given up their checking accounts and become addicted to ATM's. Then there are others who can write anything without getting fixated on one letter, but every time they open their mouths nearly nothing but nonstop, narrow narrative.

We help each other out. We talk about our addiction to alliteration but have renamed it addiction to sound-alikes so as not to get going again. We have sponsors. My sponsor was hooked on tongue twisters she'd learned as a child: Sally sells seashells by the seashore, Peter Piper picked a peck of pickled peppers. She's been clean now for almost three years.

AA is not a perfect program. Instead of alliterating we find other less hideous habits in which to indulge. We drink lots of coffee and smoke like chimneys. Keeping our mouths otherwise occupied helps us not get started on the same sound sickness - oops, sorry - I mean on the craving to alliterate. Thank goodness caffeine and tobacco have been found to have absolutely no addictive properties!

MEN - A PAUSE

To the list of things you were never told as a girl, add this: if you're single in your forties or fifties, menses may not be the only part of your life coming to an end. You may also experience a cessation of men.

A few years ago *Time* published a cover story about women in their thirties. The gist of the article was that in this age range women were more likely to be killed by terrorists than to get married. I'd say that makes my chances of marrying at fifty statistically equivalent to being killed not just by terrorists but terrorists from another planet!

During the years between my thirties and fifty, I may have lost any remnants of statistical advantage, but I have also gained. In my forties I gained the three W's that are utterly unattractive to men: weight, wisdom and (as Elmer Fudd would say) winkles.

A woman on *Oprah* once said, "To attract a higher quality man gain ten pounds." A man who loves you when you *don't* resemble a model is probably more worth being with than someone who loves you only when and if you *do.* When I kept my 5'9" body in size 8-10 clothes, men were never in short supply. But as I've gone to a size 12-14, the number of men taking notice has dwindled.

Needless to say, the "winkles" taking up "wesidence" in my face and hands contribute to my shrinking supply of dashing suitors. Like their dress shirts, men seem to want their women starched and pressed.

Wisdom is the third commodity I seem to have plenty of but men don't seem to be seeking in a woman. Along with increased wisdom, my level of confidence has soared, another trait that's not exactly a male magnet. I notice that men are more taken with tentative women. To match their girlish bodies they want malleable minds.

I sound a bit scornful you think. Why? I think I cope with "men - a pause" as well as any self-respecting, single fifty-year-old woman. I gnash my teeth, buy battery-operated equipment for the bedroom and write slightly cynical essays.

SEASONS, SIZES, SAMPLERS AND STILLS

MINNESOTA SEASONS

I'm a sucker for seasons. Granted, there are springs when the snow's still flying that I entertain fantasies of moving to Florida or Fresno, but I've never acted on them. I'm hooked on the happiness that cycles summon up in me.

My least favorite season is winter. In St. Paul every year there's actually a Winter Carnival to *celebrate* winter. This makes about as much sense as women organizing PMS Festivals. But even winter has its redeeming qualities. Nothing can rival a fresh snowfall, inches of bright white for my yard, a reminder of nature's efforts to equalize. Then there's the perfect pink of my cheeks as I come home after a brisk winter walk.

Spring is the most magical. It lavishes upon us the gift of green. No monochrome merits more praise. Its thousand shades are exquisite enough in themselves but even more so in their meaning. They *mean* growth. After months of the sterile chill of winter, everything in the world of flora begins again. Spring's the season all about newness and freshness and the lengthening of days. Everything's full of desire to reach full potential.

Summer is the season that means all things are possible. Potential is fully realized, unfurled in a thousand different ways. In a warm and sunny world our senses become sated with the sights, sounds and scents we're given for just this brief time.

Autumn is bittersweet. We know it to be a prelude to winter, the season which makes of absences a powerful presence. So autumn's when I most work at mastering the pleasure of the present moment, of living in the here and now. It's my favorite season, when colorful leaves sail through crisp, cool air, and land on carpets still soft and green.

S.A.D.

S.A.D. Classed a syndrome, the acronym stands for Seasonal Affect Disorder. Having done a little self-diagnosis, I can definitely declare that I've got it. I had it before it had a name, have it now, will probably carry it to the crematorium with me.

This syndrome has to do with the effects of sun deprivation. It occurs in the winter when the sun is a sparse commodity. If you want to know whether you have this affliction, take this simple test. Three or more yesses indicate trouble.

1. Two sunless days and it's hard liquor for breakfast, lunch, dinner, as well as midmeal snacks.

2. There's a complete correlation between cloudy skies and Tammy-Faye-Baker-style sobbing sessions.

3. You'd give your Minnesota mansion to charity, move into a trailer in Nashville just to see the sun after four P.M.

4. By mid-January you've considered grand theft larceny, proceeds to go towards a one-way ticket to Tampa and a house on the beach.

I'm four-for-four and a Minnesotan, which is almost redundant. I live in a state that selected six as the number of months a year to have the dismal season known as winter. This way you're not surprised when the skies dump twenty-six inches of snow on you on Halloween or wind chills dip below zero in April. In a month when Washington D. C. boasts cherry blossoms, we host chilly blossoms, delicate crocuses and tulips heard to mutter obscenities beneath their faint breaths, which they can frequently see.

If in Minnesota you're not suffering from some degree of S.A.D. syndrome, you're probably stricken with either T.P.P (Too Perky to Protest) or T.L.L. (Too Lutheran to Lament). Both groups give me hives. My dermatologist always marvels at their uniqueness, each red splotch resembling a miniature Minnesota. Arguably not in the same league as stigmata, they do, however, seem worthy of The Guinness Book of Records. They're my peculiar reaction to Minnesota Nice and Minnesota No No, a potent form of Nordic denial. This topical dermatitis would disappear if I trooped off to the tropics.

Needless to say, I'm ecstatic when spring comes. You can hear my Meg Ryan-like outbursts from the delicatessen scene in *When Harry Met Sally;* but I'm not faking it. I'm crazy about spring's lengthening days and its generous light. No longer hibernating, I emerge from lamp-lit days and therapeutic sessions at my local tanning center. Ancient Egyptians worshiped the sun. Is there any possibility of working a little of this into Lutheran liturgy?

ONE SIZE FITS ALL

On the rare occasion that I wear pantyhose, I make sure the pair I put on actually fits. Most manufacturers have done away with their one-size-fits-all. In the past I bought these because they were less expensive. Since I'm 5 foot 9, however, they were not a bargain. I always found myself dealing with the CD Factor, the Crotch Discrepancy Factor. The pantyhose crotch arrived and remained roughly an inch and a half above my knees. Between its crotch and mine I could easily have housed a covey of quail.

A variation on the one-size-fits-all concept is the one-style- fits-all phenomenon. Interested in getting into public speaking, I joined a local speakers' association. The first meeting of the year was scheduled for a Saturday morning. Having never attended a meeting before, I could only guess at how people would be dressed. I guessed casual. Public speakers are required to dress up for speaking engagements. Since this wasn't a speaking engagement, I assumed people would jump at the chance to dress comfortably. Wrong!

I walked into the meeting in my cotton knit top and slacks and wished immediately that some huge vacuum-gizmo could suck me back out the door.

Of the thirty or so men, all but three were dressed in suits and ties. I don't mean sport coats and slacks, I mean suits (some three-piece) and ties. Of the fifty or so women, all but four were dressed equally to the nines in their power suits, pumps and jewelry.

At the meeting everybody smiled a lot while they talked. I felt like I was in the midst of a high-powered congeniality competition. Sincerity didn't seem to be a criterion, just flashing a lot of white a lot of the time.

In the end this stiff, formal look and insincere smiling exhausted me. I vowed never to go back unless I'd been taking megadoses of vitamins and gotten at least fourteen hours sleep. Even then I thought it might be the slightest bit daunting. I broke my vow and managed to make it to one more meeting. In my comfy cotton clothes, smiling only when I felt like it, I fended off the silliness of power suits and power smiling by reminding myself that one style does not fit all!

A WHITMAN'S SAMPLER

As a child I thought the best the world of candy had to offer was the Whitman's Sampler. Close your eyes for a moment and envision the box covered in a rich, buttery yellow. The trademark cross-stitch design forms its delicate border. In the middle more of the familiar pattern displays a basket of brightly colored pansies with the word "Whitman's" crossing its path in elegant calligraphy. Inside the box lays a double layer of assorted chocolates, each piece gently held in its own miniature, tightly pleated, brown cup.

To me the best part of the Whitman's Sampler is the guide inside the lid - a marvelous treasure map of the two tiers of treats that reside below. Clearly identifying each sweet, the map distinguishes caramels from nougats and points the way to creamy centers. It eliminates guesswork and disappointment as you prepare your palate for your favorite fillings.

Yes, Whitman's Sampler was the perfect box of candy for a little girl seeking predictable pleasure. An annual gift from a far away aunt, it only appeared in our house at Christmastime. The rest of the year I had to deal with the disappointment of sinking my teeth into the unknown with candy by Fannie Farmer or Russell Stover, second class creators when it came to chocolates.

The Whitman's map showed me the lay of the land without any pressure to select one piece of candy over another. Using it, I made informed choices. Depending on my distinct desires for different tastes on my tongue and textures for my teeth, I chose one of the chocolate jewels. Someone at Whitman's long ago must have realized how reassuring it was to discover the lovely lid insert.

It's carried over into my adult life, this keen passion for predictability in my choices, especially in people. I pick what I call mapped people for friends and lovers. Mapped people are authentic. They know what their centers are made of and aren't afraid to let you know. The pleasure they bring me is reminiscent of my long ago love affair with Whitman's buttery-yellow box of chocolates.

KALEIDOSCOPE STILLS

A kaleidoscope comes with no instructions. There are some instruments we intuitively know how to use, and this is one of them. Its only purpose is to give pleasure. The telescope and microscope, distant cousins, are more eager to make the eyes work. Because of them we cure disease and discover distant stars. A kaleidoscope, on the other hand, is simply an invitation to experience wonder.

It's all achieved with such simple tools: small bits of colored glass and mirrors. Nothing expensive or extraordinary is required to create a few moments of magic. All the viewer needs is one willing, able eye. There are *no other* requirements. You can be any size, age, race, sexual preference. You can live in the tropics or Tibet, the desert or Duluth. Just bring with you a good eye and a desire to be dazzled and you're in for some pure pleasure.

The irony is that this humble cylinder couples utter randomness with strict symmetry. The randomness of how the bits of glass fall and the symmetry produced by tiny mirrors make for the odd couple of scopedom. I set the bits of glass into motion, then stop to savor the kaleidoscope still set before me. My eye takes in the brilliance and complexity of the composition, each a momentary, miniature work of art.

MEGAMALLS, MELANIN AND MEN

MEGAMALL, MEGABYTES, MEGAHERTZ

It's called the Mega Mall, and it's the largest edifice erected to crass consumerism anywhere in the world. Plane loads of Japanese tourists spend fifteen *hours* in cramped quarters just to get the chance to "shop til they drop" in a mall the size of New Jersey.

My home is less than fifteen *minutes* from the mall. My first trip there was about six months after it opened when my parents were visiting from Iowa and wanted to see it. While waiting for my mom outside a bathroom in Bloomingdale's, I started chatting with Cathy, another woman waiting. She told me she was from Mason City, Iowa, a three-hour drive from the mall, and this was her third visit. When she asked me how far away I lived and how often I'd been here, I rendered her speechless with my response. "Seven minutes and never." From her reaction, I'm surprised she didn't call security, since I'd clearly proven I was deranged. When my mom came out of the bathroom, Cathy checked her out carefully. Perhaps she was wondering whether the weirdo behavior gene came from her or my dad.

The Mega Mall is one of our modern tributes to hugeness. Somehow we've gotten way off track. We use size as some kind of measuring stick of quality or worth. I find the Guinness Book of Records informative in a silly, willy-nilly sort of way, but it's not the source I check when I'm looking for examples of true greatness.

What gets lost for me when I walk through the Mega Mall is my sense of belonging. Completely dwarfed by the size, I feel less important and connected than when I'm strolling through the small "mom and pop" shops in my neighborhood.

I'll leave the mega counting and construction to others. Mega means million and whether it applies to computer bytes, electromagnetic frequency hertz or square footage of a mall, it's all a little overwhelming to me. For me mega bites, mega hurts. Give me underwhelming any day!

TAN

I tan easily, without tanning lotion or the tedium of long hours baking in the sun. It's not the result of disciplined meditation, an iron will or great karma. Mostly it's about the amount of melanin in my skin, which creates an olive tone eager to darken at the drop of a summer straw hat (as long as the hat is dropped in a bright midday sun.)

For years I reveled in this annual, superficial transformation. People pay close attention to the shading and shaping of human skin. Both are important criteria in our concepts of beauty, as well as the borders of our bigotry. I found it intriguing that when my tan became very dark, causing me to look like I'd crossed over into another racial group, whites didn't come up with the accolades they did two shades lighter.

In my mid-twenties I counseled one summer at a junior high girls' camp (the eighth or ninth ring of hell, depending on where you rank root canal surgery). One of the girls in my tent said I looked like Dianne Carroll. I'd have regarded it a high compliment if I hadn't considered the source, which was Michelle, puberty's prickly princess of innuendo. If you could have heard her tone, seen her eyes, you'd have known that contained in the remark was the ugly seed of racism. The implication was that even though Dianne Carroll was beautiful, she was, after all, still black and black can never be as beautiful as white. Not yet versed in the art of assertiveness, I didn't retort with a clever, caustic response. Today I would give Michelle a passionate piece of my mind.

I gave up excessive tanning a number of years ago when the prune patrol (American Medical Association) came out with a strong suggestion that we eat them instead of imitate them. Limitless leisure spent in the increasingly unfiltered rays of the sun, doctors warned, would turn your skin to leather.

Also, your chances of contracting skin cancer rise to the kind of odds you pray for when shooting craps in Vegas. With my lighter look comes a chance of increased longevity sans the look of Libby the Lizard. What has not changed, though, is my personal preference for tones in the Dianne or Denzel range.

WANTED: CARNIVORES WHO CARESS

In the fifties we little girls were encouraged to aim high in our search for Mr. Right: high enough income for a suburban split level, high enough sperm count for 2.4 children to accessorize it.

This is no longer a comprehensive package. I want something else. My mother says the man who could make me happy hasn't been born yet. What can I say? My single life is good. If I'm going to give up that life it will be for someone extraordinary. Looking now for the fifties version of Mr. Right would be like settling for the $2000 deductible in a health insurance plan when what you really want is the co-pay plan. For some 20 years now I've been looking for Mr. Co-pay Man.

I'd like a man who is willing and able to put in and take out of a relationship about the same that I am - that goes for both quality and quantity. I want a peer versus a protector, an emoter versus an earner. Don't get me wrong here. If I'm being attacked by bats, I clearly would like him on the spot wielding a broom and an attitude. And I don't want someone who's home surfing the soaps while I'm bringing home the bacon. But these criteria to me are just common sense. Hopefully he'd want me to be broom-wielding (if bats had suddenly made *him* the center of their universe) and earning my own way, too.

Okay, you say it's too much to expect, but in the emotional realm I want Mr. Right to be a highly evolved peer as well: someone who's honest and open, has a full range of emotions, and an awareness of feelings and the willingness to communicate.

Well, right about now you likely are agreeing with my mom that I am just the slightest bit picky. You're probably right, but so what. I have no intention of surrendering to pressure. And just in case you thought the laborious list was complete, let me add a little more weight to my sinking ship on its journey in search of the Co-pay Guy.

I'm looking for a balance I've finally found in myself between being and doing, thinking and feeling, gentleness and firmness. To everything there is a season. Give me a man with a four-season range. This man can sink his teeth into a great meal of ribs and, after we've done the dishes together, enjoy the pleasures of caressing. Give me a man with a generous heart, adept hands and a great set of incisors! Is that really too much to ask?

DON'T FENCE ME IN

THE SMILING DISEASE

From magazine covers and beauty pageants to saccharine sitcoms we're urged to SMILE, SMILE, SMILE. There are few exceptions to this dental dictum. Smiling is the language in which we're expected to be fluent. Speak it with your children, your husband or boyfriend, your co-workers, your boss, your neighbors. And if, God forbid, aggressive aliens should abduct you, politely flash your pearly whites as they drag you off to the mother ship. You are, after all, their guest.

The smiling expectation extends to most functions we find ourselves forging or foraging through. Be it piano recitals, wedding receptions, or parent-teacher conferences for the kid who's prone to acting out, we're expected to expose a generous amount of oral gleam.

Don't get me wrong. I'm all for smiling *when it's spontaneous and real*. A conditioned reflex designed solely to attract or please, though, is more like a disease. Someone totally taken with the SMILE, SMILE, SMILE code of compliance is hardly the picture of mental health and well-being. Incessant smiling is hazardous to your health!

By now you're no doubt aware that I don't subscribe to the "Pack up your troubles in your old kit bag and SMILE, SMILE, SMILE" school of thought. In my experience, troubles don't pack well. They're neither soft and malleable like cotton security blankets nor small and compact like reassuring travel alarms.

Troubles are more like a pickup load full of defunct home appliances. They're heavy, take up lots of space and serve no useful function. Don't pack these puppies in your old kit bag and proceed to smile. Instead, get help from friends or professionals who are well-versed in proper procedures for transferring tonnage.

Don't smile while loading them onto the truck or off it at the nearest salvage yard. A "smile while" policy only increases your chances of a hernia. Instead, save the smile for afterwards when it's an authentic response to the joy of completing a difficult task!

DIRECTIONS

"**D**irections." This ambitious word can indicate the north, south, east, and west of maps, globes, the entire physical world through which we wend our way. It can refer to the geographic guiding of one person by another, as in "giving" directions. Of course, giving directions must follow asking for assistance, an event most males avoid like proctologists or the plague. Directions come with board games and bicycles with "some assembly required" (translation: make no other plans for the weekend).

Inherent in any definition of directions is guidance, being navigated or steered to a place or an end. Different groups assign different value to directions. The military, for instance, forms its entire foundation on the notion that following *orders* (the Arnold Schwartzenegger of directions) is essential. If you're not firmly convinced that taking orders is an admirable action, don't consider an armed services career.

Again and again I'm amazed at how widespread the desire to give and take directions is. From preachers to politicians, gurus to gynecologists, there are hosts of "leaders" available to those hoards anxious for guidance - to be told what to think and do. Some promise a kind of wholesale happiness while others lure you in with the math of miracles (three simple steps to this, seven easy steps to that). I do best when I take a little from here, a little from there. Eventually I come up with what fits the curves and angles of the actual me.

WIDTH

Some say it's our sense of humor, others our ability to reason and plan. I say that what really separates us humans, plops us in a place apart from others in the animal kingdom, is our mania for measuring. Give a species a set of opposable thumbs and one of the first tools you get after weapons and utensils is something with notches on it.

Where did this preoccupation with "sizing up" come from? I have no idea. What I do know is that my favorite dimension, my favorite measurement, is width. An old Mexican proverb proclaims "life is short but it's wide." The first time I read the aphorism I was alone in my study. Sitting in my Danish Modern chair, I felt a broad, appreciative grin forming on my face as I pondered the magnificence of Mexican wisdom. This image strikingly opposes the restraint and repression that emerges from another metaphor, walking the straight and narrow. At that moment I experienced the pleasure of a perfect proverb.

Acknowledging that life is wide is freeing. The straight and narrow always felt a little claustrophobic to me. The walls were too close, the air stifling. Added width offers me added wealth. Life is rich with choices, possibilities - a myriad of ways to both be and behave. Added width gives me more psychic space to move around, to make some memorable mistakes, to try again or not. It's all up to me.

The proverb I'm so passionate about now hangs above my desk in that same study where I first discovered it. I fashioned the words in a kind of wild and wonderful calligraphy, matted them in passionate purple. Passion is still what I feel when my eyes catch the strong, simple saying hovering over my desk like a benediction.

DUPED BY DISNEY

Some of you, a little nervous about the title, are thinking, "Is nothing sacred? Is she going to find fault with a sacred standard that's been synonymous with entertainment and delight for children for over fifty years?" Well, in a word, yes.

There's nothing wrong with the *concept* of entertaining children through animation and song, even gigantic theme parks. It's the *content* that troubles me. If you examine closely what Disney Studios create, you'll acknowledge their perpetuation of a double standard for little boys and little girls.

Certainly you've noticed the uncanny resemblance of Disney heroines to Barbie dolls. If you translate the proportions of Barbie into human size, this woman's measurements would be in the area of 42-18-34. Don't you agree such measurements are a little daunting as a heroine for little girls?

But, you protest, Disney heroes are equally unrealistic physically. Let's consider the princes in Cinderella, Snow White, and Sleeping Beauty. Yes, in these animated films the heroes are as goofy-looking as the heroines. In these stories the double standard is not in appearance but in what I call "access to action." The females become princesses through passivity. Their only challenge to action is in the area of appearance. The message is make sure you *do* everything you possibly can to look good and to be noticed. Be sure you're in the right place at the right time so the prince can see you. In these seemingly harmless tales, these heroines limit their aspirations to acquisition of the prince and the palace. I'd like a little wider range of dreams for our daughters and grand-daughters.

And then there's the whole double standard played out in such classics as Beauty and the Beast. The lesson we supposedly learn is to look beyond the external when searching for true beauty. I don't quarrel with the lesson, only its lopsided application. Why is it always the female discovering this wisdom? How about a Beauty and the Beast where *he's* the beauty, she's the beast? The fact that this may seem ludicrous only goes to show how entrenched the double standard is.

If I had an afternoon when I could schmooze with the boys at Disney, I'd tell them how *creative* their animation is, how *clever* their songs are, how *clean* their theme parks are. Then I'd ask them to add to their repertoire of admirable adjectives the "f" word: fairness. I'd encourage them to use that creativity and cleverness (the obsessive cleanliness being optional) to create stories where both genders engage in a full range of activities and emotional expression, where being human is more important than meeting some arbitrary idea of what's masculine and feminine.

MAKEOVERS

One of the most familiar ratings grabbers on daytime TV is what's referred to as the makeover. Someone is selected from the studio audience or from applications sent in by viewers at home. The "lucky woman" is treated to a day of superficial transformation.

The assumption is that the audience will excitedly ooh and ah over the "new woman" created by beauticians, make-up artists and clothing consultants. Sometimes I do ooh and ah, but other times a perfectly wonderful, natural-looking woman has been transformed not into someone more beautiful but simply someone more keenly committed to the shallow.

With a makeover, the decision has been made to financially and functionally complicate a person's life. The originally lovely looking woman must now make a commitment to purchase and to preen. She'll have to dole out dollars for hair color, makeup, a certain style of clothing, but payment won't end there. At the toll booth of "beauty" she'll also have to tender her time, unless she also wins the lottery and can afford to hire an entourage to coif, clothe and cosmeticize her every morning.

A close cousin to the TV makeover is the photography business known as Glamour Shots. Totally targeted at women, the underlying message seems to be that flaunting and floozylike portrait poses are what men go wild for in their women.

I'm not so much disputing the assumption as I am refusing to succumb to it unless the guys reciprocate.

A little equality only seems sensible. If I'm going to get decked out in boas and beads the least my guy can do is go for a little leather and lotion. Personally, I've always preferred a little more substance when I'm searching for sexiness (i.e. a brain, a heart and a good sense of humor), but I'm comfortable leaning into a good lapse now and then.

WEARING PURPLE

Are you familiar with the poem "When I Am an Old Woman I Shall Wear Purple?" The basic premise, if you aren't, is that old age will free you up to be bolder, less cautious. When I first read that poem it was clear to me that I'd started "old woman" behavior when I was in my thirties, after my divorce.

My wardrobe didn't suddenly turn totally purple, but vivid colors did start popping up. In addition to the purple, hot pink, royal blue and bright turquoise joined the beiges and pastels. Opening my closet door turned into a little venture in viewing variety.

I freed up in other ways, too. In addition to breaking through the boredom barrier in color, I began wearing sassy caps and doing standup comedy. For most people doing standup ranks right up there with bungi jumping. I delighted in this daring new pursuit.

My fear of bringing attention to myself decreased. I didn't go over some narcissistic edge, suddenly turn into Miss Piggy, but I did start seeing attention on me as legitimate as attention on anyone else.

You could say I also developed quite a mouth. I began saying what was on my mind. Needless to say, this didn't meet with universal approval. Frequently, it was met with a "mouth response" from others, a severe dropping of the jaw in disbelief.

This "gaping mouth" response fell into two categories: seeing me as simply having no self-restraint or seeing me as not being very nice. In the land of "Minnesota Nice" this latter offense falls just short of criminal. I think it's just a matter of time before our state legislature comes up with ordinances mandating niceness. I can foresee the day I'll be booked for being bold.

But I've grown fond of my mouth, its bold and sassy ways. I might even be willing to do a little time in the "big house" for speaking out. It feels great to get things off my brightly clad chest.

If you've read the purple poem and plan to put a little boldness and passion in your life when you're eighty, I urge you to reevaluate. Consider the possibility of now!

CHANGE

Remember the "change-a-light-bulb" riddles? My favorite one went like this: How many therapists does it take to change a light bulb? Just one, but the light bulb has to *really* want to change.

Change is the one constant in life, but most of us stubbornly and stalwartly resist it. We like a little loose change in our pockets, but getting loose and relaxed about change in our lives is a completely different matter. A friend of mine travelling through a small town in southern Iowa before an election came upon a billboard that simply read VOTE NO FOR CHANGE. A lot of us are carrying that sign around internally, even if we don't have it plastered on the bumpers of our cars or splashed across our front lawns. Most of us don't *really* want to change.

I'm German, so change held about as much charm for me as a case of athlete's foot. For a long time my two favorite words in the entire English language were controlling and cleaning. Controlling and cleaning, cleaning and controlling. Those were the only two kinds of change I wanted to see: one where I played the potent puppet-master pulling all the strings or one that involved a lot of scrubbing walls, waxing floors and beating mattresses.

Some of you not familiar with the German way of life may think the beating of mattresses is part of some kinky S & M ritual. Rest assured it is not. When I was young, springtime meant hauling the mattresses off all the beds and schlepping them outside. We then beat out of them all the filthy (and brace yourselves here, because I'm about to use a four-letter word) dust - yes, beat out of them all the voluminous, dastardly dust which had been allowed to accumulate in our German mattresses for a year.

Besides being German, I'm also a Virgo, which is almost redundant. Virgos love three things: organizing, controlling and cleaning. We Virgos aren't necessarily against spontaneity . . . as long as it's well thought out ahead of time. Spontaneity for me pretty much meant going to the supermarket without having typed the grocery list . . . alphabetically . . . on lined paper.

Even with all of this German and Virgo in me, in my thirties change became, as Martha Stewart would chirp, "a good thing." Choosing the difficult change of divorce heralded for me the beginning of a love affair with change. In my circle of friends I'm now known for ushering in change - from frequent furniture rearrangement and job switching to ever-changing wardrobe shifts. I invite change to add exhilarating dimensions and drama to my life.

PAST, PRESENT, FUTURE

PASSIONATE PROTEST

Steven was a dead ringer for Huck Finn, with huge, blue eyes, a generous sprinkling of freckles and a sense of adventure that could easily have commandeered a raft down the mighty Mississip. He was without a doubt my favorite first grader that first year I taught. Unfortunately, the non-fiction of his home life portrayed a harsh reality. Although his single, young mother struggled to make ends meet with Steven and an infant, eventually the stresses and strains pushed her over the emotional edge. Steven went to live with a foster family, which meant he had to attend another school. Losing him broke my heart.

The four months I had with him created a lasting impression. Perhaps because of his bare bones and disruptive home life, Steven's fiction (passed off as fact) turned life into a whopping adventure. He invented stories of swimming with alligators and riding wild tigers in which his vivid imagination accompanied a righteous indignation that often stopped me dead in my tracks.

Steven, along with all my first graders, ate lunch in a huge room with hundreds of other kids. The acoustics were terrible and supervision minimal. They'd return to the classroom restless and rattled. To calm them down I'd darken the room by pulling down the shades and play soothing music or a story record.

One day I played the story of Snow White and the Seven Dwarfs. As usual, Steven listened intently. When the wicked queen cackled "I'm going to kill Snow White with this poison apple" Steven stood straight up, pounded his fist on his desk and shouted, "Oh, no you're not!"

I still sometimes think about Steven - his flare for drama, his passionate sense of justice - and I wonder whether either survived. When I am a witness to someone being treated unfairly, I enlist Steven's tactic and hurl words of protest into the air, into the ears of anyone who will listen.

PUSH TO START

When my son, Wayne, was seven, he and I made one of our weekly trips to the grocery store. As usual, we put our bags in the trunk, and settled into our little Capri. This time, when I tried to start the car, the engine wouldn't turn over. After repeated efforts failed, we headed to the service station across the street for help. Trudging back to our ailing auto, we escorted a mechanic who opened the hood and started tinkering.

My curious son shadowed his every move. Suddenly, his keen eyes came upon something overlooked by both adults, a small, red button inscribed with the command: PUSH TO START. Even after he pointed it out to us, the mechanic and I were skeptical of such a simple solution. Undeterred by our distrust, Wayne pushed the button and the car started.

Sometimes we make things more complicated than they have to be. Life is full of complexities. Anyone who's ever attempted to do their own taxes or program their VCR knows this. But because we live in a world where so much *is* complicated and confusing, this assumption sometimes spills over to areas where it's not.

During the process of writing this book, I learned my most recent lesson in simplicity. In my usual, overly analytical style, I labored over a list of all I needed to do to write this book: gain support from friends; read books on writing a book; uncover writing blocks through therapy; create a writing schedule.

In the midst of all this list making and procrastinating, I had a date with my daughter, Kim, to celebrate her birthday. Over curried chicken salad in her cozy living room Kim told me of a psychic reading she'd recently done. Since we share skepticism of this kind of thing, I reacted with surprise and curiosity. As she reported what this psychic said, I couldn't believe how much of it rang true. Like Kim, my initial doubts faded as more and more information fit.

Kim asked about all the significant relationships in her life. After commenting on our mother-daughter relationship the psychic commented that the spirits were a little frustrated with me, that I'd been wanting to do something for several years now, but that I was fighting within myself and not getting it done. Through her the spirits wanted to tell me that this project was important and that it was time now to "just do it."

I was stunned. The immediate reaction was to crack a joke about the spirits evidently being the "Nike Spirits," but on some profound level I knew this to be an accurate account of what I'd been doing. What I needed to do to complete this book was to abandon my list and everything on it. Instead, I needed to get up every day, go to my writing desk and WRITE!

Just do it! I focus on those three powerful words when I start veering, procrastinating, creating reasons why not to write this book. And the book *is* getting written! Sometimes life is so simple.

FUTURE TENSE

I attended college in the sixties at a Baptist liberal arts school with only a thousand students. It was small and safe. Although I was living away for the first time, in many ways this haven was merely an extension of home life.

My school occupied one city block in a quiet residential area of St. Paul. Loving my cloistered life, I rarely ventured off campus. While others my age were experimenting with drugs and protesting the war, I was attending chapel and practicing chastity. When graduation finally rolled around, facing the future in the big wide world made my sequestered little psyche tense.

Since then I've discovered that "future tense," as I call this fear of the future, is not that uncommon. As tense-hopping goes (present to past, present to future) the jumping backwards is easier. Look at the fascination people have with nostalgia. Nostalgia drives the sale of everything from bucolic antiques to the Beatles anthology. On the Richter scale of time travel, reminiscing registers as safer. It is less jolting than jumping into the uncharted future.

To put it in math terms, the past is a known quantity. It's already happened. We *recognize* it when we see it in pictures, hear or read its words woven into stories. Recognition instills a level of comfort impossible to experience with the unrecognized, the unknown.

A couple of years ago my daughter began dating someone new. As we sat in my living room talking about him, I asked what it was that attracted her to him. Her answer? "Mom, I recognize him." As she explained that some of his life experiences bore a striking similarity to her own, I realized that recognition helps us relax around another person. This is also true of another time. We are comfortable with known quantities.

However, a known quantity is not guaranteed in the future. We can't remember or recognize that which still lies ahead. I realize now that what the future *can* offer is possibility. I no longer harbor a fear of the future. It no longer makes me tense. In place of fear and tension is the more positive feeling, anticipation, popularized by Carly Simon. Anticipation carries with it excitement and keen interest. Now for me "future tense" means eager to move ahead.

OBJECT LESSONS

LAUNDRY

I grew up in a rambling, hundred-year-old house which harbored four generations of women, my great-grandmother, grandmother, mother and me. We all played a part in the process called laundry. Like many domestic duties, it was endless. Even before the last shirt dried on the line someone was tossing a soggy towel or dirty socks into a recently emptied hamper.

In the days before dryers, we hung everything out on the clothes line in the back yard to dry. I nostalgically remember hauling out wicker baskets heavy with wet clothes, sheets and towels, fragrant with the scent of Tide. To keep the pieces in place, wooden, sun-bleached clothespins perched on the laundry of our lives like rows of proud juncos.

Without knowing it, I was practicing a kind of backyard Buddhism, its focused reverence on the ordinary. Hanging up and taking down laundry taught me the full, fine pleasure and solace of simple tasks. I learned to immerse myself in the moment with its lively scenario. Flitting birds chirped, vivid colors waved, a fresh scent wafted, and everything from thick, nubby towels to sheer, gauzy blouses grazed the sensitive tips of my fingers. Steeped in this stirring sphere of the senses, I began acquiring a "taste" for the sensual in a back yard brimming with it.

THE BALL AND THE BAG

While attending a workshop on creative problem-solving I was struck by one particular example placed before us. The problem involved a young golfer who on the sixteenth hole was positioned to take the lead in a prestigious tournament. He'd placed his first shot close to the green, thereby giving him a good chance to birdie the hole and pull into the lead by a shot. The problem was that somehow a small paper bag had blown onto the fairway, and the ball had landed in the bag. If the golfer removed the ball from the bag he'd take a penalty stroke. If he hit the ball while still in the bag, it would be a very poor shot. Either way, he could kiss his chances to birdie the hole goodbye. What, our facilitator asked, could be done to solve this problem?

After giving us a few minutes to ponder this, no one came up with an answer. The facilitator then told us that the solution was burning the bag. I was stunned. My thoughts as I'd tried to solve the problem had been on *moving* matter (getting the ball out of the bag or the bag away from the ball) while the solution lay in *transforming* matter. It's a mistake I've made before. Movement always seems simpler, safer than transformation.

This is not true for young children. When her son was three, a friend of mine was walking with him past the

Minnesota governor's mansion. In the yard stood a marble statue of an angel. Cautioning her son that they could look at it from the sidewalk but not go up and touch it, he exclaimed, "You don't want me to touch it because you know I can make it alive!" My friend's fear of trespassing had been interpreted by her son as a fear of transformation.

Why are we so reluctant to burn bags on the fairway or bring stone angels to life? Why, as a species, are we so cautious? Caution has its place, but when it becomes the *prime* factor in problem solving we become stodgy and safe, followed by predictable and dull.

JACKS

Games are universal. Every culture, from the most elementary to the most elevated, recognizes the need for play. Games I played as a child return as vivid, valued memories. I loved most the ones competitive in a cordial, friendly way the ones with not much at stake in winning or losing, certainly not our sense of self-worth.

When I was very young my favorite game was jacks. I played with my best friend, Barb, who lived two houses down from me. What I don't recall about playing this game is who was better, who won more. What's memorable are the reddish-orange color of the small, spongy ball, its equatorial seam, the tiny knobs on the tips of the silver jacks to protect our tender palms. I recall the rhythm of gently throwing the ball into the air, quickly scooping up the jacks before the ball bounced. The rhythm of your turn, my turn, of alternating the spotlight added a sense of equality and fairness.

In playing jacks we sized down our world, but in this context it was a positive thing. It didn't create the kind of resentment that accompanies someone else deciding *for* you to close in the walls. Barb and I *chose* this focus on the details of dexterity, moments spent managing the movement of a small ball and softly spiked jacks. The desire to win was never deadly. It never cancelled out the joy of time shared with a friend, hands happily repeating the actions of holding on, letting go of the treasured objects of this familiar game.

TANGLES

I live near a lovely, historic section of Minneapolis called Tangletown, which got its name from its disorderly web of winding streets. Lacking the calming clarity of perpendicular, gridlike neighborhoods, it's nevertheless a charming part of the city, with its lovely, rambling homes and a picturesque creek running through it. The tangle can be part of the charm if you just accept it.

There are, of course, other types of tangles. One summer when my children were very young, our family headed off to a week-long church camp in the North Woods. The idyllic setting boasted a vast, shimmering lake, a rustic lodge and a luscious expanse of green lawn. Our first day there I was on that lawn with Diane and John, working to untangle some string and twine that were going to be used for macrame. As John worked on a particularly challenging nest of knots he commented: "You know, this is like some peoples' lives."

Laughing a soft, superior laugh, I remember feeling sorry for people whose lives were a mass of tangles. At the same time, I was absolutely certain my own life would never turn into such gnarled complexity. Metaphorically, I considered my life a carefully constructed piece of macrame.

It's been twenty-five years since I laughed that smug laugh, and I can tell you knotless construction is next to impossible. At times my life has become a jumble of disorderly tangles and knots.

An important distinction I've learned to make is between tangles that need to be undone and those that don't. The first I go after with my own blend of patience and panache, and the latter I take pleasure in following down their unique, winding pathways.

BOOKMARKS

Lacking an acquisitive nature, I'll never be a true collector. However, if I'm suddenly overcome one day with an overwhelming urge to collect, the objects of my obsession will be bookmarks. I love their modest dimensions, doing what they need to do with only two. Their simple purpose of marking a place is important, helping the reader in her journey through pages of passion or poetry or paleontology.

Too small to be called a collection, I do, however, possess an assortment of bookmarks. They lie in a desk drawer and stand in pottery pencil holders, an eclectic assortment in color and content, texture and type. One measures two inches wide and is a combination of technology and handiwork. Glued to heavy blue paper is a sheet of white with a red cardinal, blue pines and a poem called *Christmas.* My friend Pam created both the poem and the bookmark. I treasure it for its well-crafted words, for Pam's caring acts of making it and presenting it to me as a gift.

Another contains words of wisdom from the writer Brenda Ueland, but I spurn it because of its turquoise and yellow colors, its ornately scrolled border and its laminated slickness. Consequently, it stands erect and glossy in one of my pencil holders, picked up only occasionally so that I can re-read the strong and wise words.

Pam's is my widest bookmark, but not my thickest. That distinction goes to one I acquired at a University of Iowa dinner. It's fringed, pliable leather is in the school colors, black and gold. Sitting at our table was the sister of an acclaimed Twin Cities poet. Discovering our common interest we lost ourselves in an evening of engaging conversation. Every time I hold this malleable marker in my hand I remember this magical evening.

My favorite bookmarks pale (literally, not figuratively) when compared to the others. I picked up three of them when buying books at The Hungry Mind Bookstore. They're a soft gray and measure only one inch by four. The paper stock is perfect, having enough weight to feel sturdy without crossing the line to a kind of stubborn stiffness. Maybe that's why I love them. It's like being so taken with a friend or lover because of one strong, shining trait they possess - a genuine laugh, deep integrity or a complete love of children.

These three little markers are the ones most frequently found in my books. The others lie and stand in waiting, wholly willing to display themselves if ever I decide to turn an affection into a collection.

GEOGRAPHY

Whether I'm gazing at photos of our blue-marble planet or at a six-year-old's map of her neighborhood, I feel a magnetic pull toward depictions of places and spaces. As a writer, this connection often appears as metaphor in my poetry and short stories.

In my children I see variations on this theme. My son, Wayne, has the uncanny ability to maintain his sense of direction in almost any unexplored territory or circumstance. Like a migratory bird, with some kind of internal compass, he guides us to our destination and home again, grappling with suspect directions and maize-like detours strewn in our path.

My daughter Kim's connection to geography takes a different form. She loves to study it. In college geography was one of her majors. She loves maps of all kinds as well as traveling far enough from home to start following the earth's subtle curvature, seeing varied land forms, singular seas, and distant skies.

A large world map covers the majority of the hallway wall of my little home. It's the Rand McNally map where Greenland is the size of North America. It hovers there in the upper central part of the map and looks like a big bully threatening to slide south at any moment, wreaking havoc on anything or anybody in its way. It never does, though; instead, it stays utterly still, a large, permanent patch of green floating in the North Atlantic.

I consult my map whenever hearing or reading about some unfamiliar country, some island or sea whose whereabouts I'm not sure of. Finding it on the map always comforts me. It's similar to the satisfaction I feel when a piece fits into a puzzle. Here the puzzle's already put together, and my only task is location.